The New Faces of Autism

Stories and Science of Neurodiversity in a Changing World

Jary Masher

COPYRIGHT

Dedication

To every individual on the autism spectrum: Your unique voices and perspectives are not only worthy of celebration but also of deep respect. This book is for you, for your strength, resilience, and the incredible ways you shape the world around us. May your journey toward self-acceptance, understanding, and belonging continue to inspire change and challenge outdated norms.

To those who love, support, and advocate for neurodivergence: Your unwavering commitment to inclusion and acceptance is a beacon of hope. Thank you for your compassion, patience, and advocacy that fuels a better future for all of us.

Contents

Dedication ----------------------------------- 3

Foreword---------------------------------------11

Introduction ---------------------------------16

What You Will Discover in This Book 19

Chapter 1 -------------------------------------22

Understanding Autism --------------------22

The Science Behind Autism: A New
Perspective -------------------------22

Neurodiversity: The New Paradigm ---24

Breaking the Myths: What Autism Is and
Isn't---26

Chapter 2 -------------------------------------28

The Spectrum and Beyond ----------------28

Beyond the Diagnostic Criteria:
Autism's Diverse Faces------------28

The Many Ways Autism Manifests ----30

Embracing the Full Spectrum ----------32

Chapter 3 -------------------------------------35

The Voices of Autism--------------------35

Personal Narratives: Real Stories from the Spectrum-----------------35

Finding Identity and Belonging--------37

Voices That Challenge the Norm-------39

Empowering Advocacy-----------------41

Chapter 4 -------------------------------------43

The Science of Neurodiversity------------43

Neurobiology of Autism: A Deeper Dive --------------------------------43

The Strengths of Neurodivergent Minds --------------------------------------45

How Neurodiversity Is Shaping Society --------------------------------------47

Scientific Breakthroughs Supporting Neurodiversity --------------------------49

Chapter 5 -------------------------------------51

The Role of Society in Shaping Autism --51

The Social Stigma: Past and Present --------------------------------------51

Shifting Perspectives: A Movement Toward Acceptance ---------------------- 53

The Role of Media, Representation, and Language --------------------------------- 55

How Society Can Foster Neurodiversity -- 57

Toward a More Inclusive Future ------- 59

Chapter 6 --------------------------------------- 60

Autism in the Workplace ------------------ 60

Autistic Strengths in Professional Environments ----------------------- 60

Navigating Workplace Challenges ----- 62

Success Stories: How Neurodiversity Drives Innovation 64

How Businesses and Organizations Benefit ------------------------------------- 66

Building a More Inclusive Workplace - 67

Chapter 7 --------------------------------------- 69

Autism in Education ----------------------- 69

Rethinking Learning: Tailoring Education for Neurodiverse Minds --69

Challenges in Traditional Education Systems ------------------------------------71

How Schools and Communities Can Be More Inclusive ------------------72

Teachers and Parents: Collaborating for Success --------------------------74

Chapter 8 --77

Autism in Relationships --------------------77

Navigating Friendships and Family Dynamics ----------------------------77

Romantic Relationships: Challenges and Insights--------------------------79

Building Strong Support Networks --80

Strategies for Strengthening Connections ------------------------81

Chapter 9 --83

The Future of Autism Awareness ---------83

Changing Perceptions and Creating Space for Neurodivergence -------83

The Role of Technology and Innovation in Autism Care ----------------------------85

The Global Movement for Neurodiversity ----------------------86

A Vision for an Inclusive Future -87

Lighting the Path Forward---------88

Conclusion ---90

Final Thoughts: Redefining What It Means to Be Autistic --------------92

Acknowledgements -------------------------94

"Autism is not a puzzle to be solved, but a spectrum of brilliance to be understood."
— JARY MASHER

The New Faces of Autism

Stories and Science of Neurodiversity in a Changing World

JARY MASHER

Foreword

Autism is often seen as a diagnosis, a label, a set of behaviors or traits that can be misunderstood or even feared. But this view overlooks something crucial: autism is not merely a condition—it's a way of being in the world. A way that, when understood and embraced, enriches all of us. This book, *The New Faces of Autism: Shaping the Future of Neurodiversity*, offers a powerful lens through which to see autism not as something to be fixed or cured, but as a part of the natural human experience that deserves understanding, respect, and, above all, acceptance.

For decades, the narrative around autism has been shaped by a medicalized, deficit-based model that focuses primarily on what people with autism cannot do, or how they are "different" in ways that make them seem less than their neurotypical peers. This book challenges that outdated mindset. It shines a light on the true diversity within the autism spectrum and introduces the idea of neurodiversity, a paradigm that recognizes differences in neurological development as natural and valuable variations of the human condition. It pushes back against myths and misconceptions, emphasizing that these differences are not deficits, but unique ways of thinking and experiencing the world that bring significant strengths and innovations.

Through the personal stories shared in this book, we hear from individuals who experience autism in vastly different ways—some may struggle with communication or sensory overload, while others might excel in fields like technology, art, or mathematics. These stories offer readers a deeper understanding of the rich complexity of the autism spectrum. These are not just stories of survival or overcoming obstacles. They are stories of thriving in environments that embrace neurodiversity, stories of finding community, acceptance, and a place to belong.

Autism is not a one-size-fits-all experience, and that is perhaps one of its greatest strengths. This book invites readers to step into the shoes of those with autism and to recognize their unique contributions to society. It also challenges us to reexamine the way we think about the world—about work, education, family, and social dynamics—and to question what it truly means to be "normal."

As the world becomes more connected, we have a greater opportunity—and responsibility—to foster inclusivity and compassion. This book isn't just about understanding autism; it's about transforming society's views and practices to embrace neurodiversity in all its forms. It's about creating spaces where everyone, regardless of their neurological makeup, can thrive. The voices and perspectives shared here—though diverse in their experiences—speak to a common truth: when we allow neurodivergence to be celebrated, we all benefit. The world is changing, and so are the ways we think about and interact with autism. The stories and research in this book represent a shift toward a more inclusive future, one where all individuals, regardless of how they learn, think, or experience life, are recognized for the value they bring.

As you read these pages, let your perspective shift. Challenge the assumptions you might have held about autism, and open your heart to a more inclusive world. The faces of autism are many, and they are all deserving of a place in the conversation. The future is one where neurodiversity is not just acknowledged but celebrated, and the journey toward this future starts now.

Jary Masher, MD

Introduction

Autism is not a single story. It's a rich mosaic of experiences, abilities, and challenges that touch lives in ways as unique as the individuals themselves. For many years, autism was seen through a narrow lens—defined largely by stereotypes, outdated science, and a lack of understanding. This book was born out of a desire to break free from those confines and paint a fuller, more authentic picture of what it means to live on the autism spectrum today.

My connection to this topic runs deep. Over the years, I've had the privilege of learning from autistic individuals—friends, family members, colleagues, and advocates—each of whom taught me something new about neurodiversity and the resilience of the human spirit. Their experiences underscored how far we've come in understanding autism but also revealed how much work remains. This book is my way of honoring their stories while contributing to the growing movement toward acceptance and inclusion.

The Changing Landscape of Autism

Autism awareness has come a long way from its beginnings. Decades ago, the term "autism" was often shrouded in mystery and misunderstanding. Diagnoses were rare, supports were limited, and society largely viewed autism as a condition to be fixed or hidden. Fast forward to today, and the narrative has shifted dramatically.

We now understand that autism exists on a spectrum—a term that reflects its incredible diversity. The spectrum isn't a linear scale of **"more"** or **"less"** autistic but a complex, multi-dimensional experience encompassing communication styles, sensory sensitivities, interests, and ways of thinking. This broader understanding has reshaped everything from diagnostic criteria to how society approaches education, work, and relationships for autistic individuals.

One of the most significant shifts has been the embrace of neurodiversity. This concept recognizes that neurological differences, such as autism, ADHD, and dyslexia, are natural variations of the human brain, not deficits. Neurodiversity celebrates the strengths that come with these differences—like creativity, focus, and unique problem-solving abilities—while acknowledging the challenges that individuals might face in navigating a world designed for neurotypical people.

Despite this progress, barriers persist. Autistic individuals often encounter stigma, misconceptions, and a lack of accommodations in environments ranging from classrooms to workplaces. This book aims to bridge the gap between awareness and meaningful change. It's not just about understanding autism; it's about fostering a world where neurodiverse people can thrive.

What You Will Discover in This Book

This book is both a guide and a conversation. It invites readers to step into the world of autism, not as outsiders looking in, but as participants in a dialogue about identity, inclusion, and understanding. Through stories, research, and practical insights, we'll explore the many faces of autism and the lessons they hold for all of us.

First, we'll unpack the science. You'll learn how autism is defined today and how its biological and neurological underpinnings influence everything from sensory processing to social interaction. But this isn't just a scientific deep dive; it's a journey into the lived experiences of autistic individuals, whose voices bring the data to life.

You'll also meet a diverse group of individuals on the spectrum—each with their own challenges, triumphs, and perspectives. Their stories remind us that autism is not a monolith. It's a vibrant, varied community filled with voices that demand to be heard. These narratives will challenge stereotypes and show how autistic individuals contribute to society in ways that are as profound as they are inspiring.

Beyond personal stories, this book examines the systems and structures that impact the autism community. From education to employment, we'll explore what's working, what isn't, and how we can do better. You'll find practical advice for creating more inclusive environments, whether in classrooms, offices, or community spaces.

What sets this book apart is its dual focus on science and storytelling. Many works on autism lean heavily toward one or the other—either diving into clinical research or centering solely on personal anecdotes. Here, we aim to strike a balance. By weaving together these elements, we provide both the data and the humanity needed to truly understand the spectrum.

Finally, this book is a call to action. It challenges readers to move beyond awareness and into advocacy. How can we create a world where autistic individuals feel seen, respected, and empowered? What role can

AUTISM ISN'T A DISABILLITY
AUTISM ISN'T A DISABILITY
AUTISM ISN'T A DISABILITY
AUTISM ISN'T A ABILLITY
AUTISMM ISN' A DISABILLITY
AUTISM ISN'T A DIFFERENT ABILITY

Chapter 1

Understanding Autism

The Science Behind Autism: A New Perspective

Autism has long been misunderstood, defined by outdated science and narrow perspectives. In the mid-20th century, autism was considered a rare and extreme condition, often diagnosed only in individuals with significant communication challenges or intellectual disabilities. The infamous "refrigerator mother" theory—claiming autism resulted from cold or unloving parenting—epitomized the damaging misconceptions of the time. Thankfully, science has moved far beyond those erroneous ideas.

Today, autism is understood as a neurodevelopmental condition with a biological basis. Advances in genetics, neuroimaging, and behavioral studies reveal that autism arises from a complex interplay of factors. While no single "cause" exists, researchers have identified patterns of brain connectivity and sensory processing that differ from those of neurotypical individuals. These differences are not flaws but variations in how the brain is wired to perceive, interpret, and interact with the world.

The concept of a spectrum is another critical development. Autism is no longer viewed as a binary condition where someone is either "autistic" or "not." Instead, the spectrum acknowledges a wide range of traits and intensities that vary from person to person. This more nuanced understanding has expanded diagnoses and allowed individuals who might have been overlooked in the past—particularly women, people of color, and those with subtler traits—to receive recognition and support.

Neurodiversity: The New Paradigm

The rise of the neurodiversity movement represents a paradigm shift in how society understands autism and other neurological differences. Coined by sociologist Judy Singer in the 1990s, the term **"neurodiversity"** posits that variations in brain function are natural and valuable, akin to biodiversity in ecosystems.

This perspective challenges the notion of autism as solely a medical diagnosis to be treated or cured. Instead, it frames autism as part of the broad spectrum of human diversity, with its own strengths, challenges, and perspectives. Neurodiversity advocates stress that society's focus should not be on changing autistic individuals but on creating environments that respect and support their needs.

For example, the intense focus and deep interests that some autistic individuals exhibit are often seen as deficits. In reality, these traits can lead to remarkable achievements in areas such as technology, art, and science. Similarly, sensory sensitivities—frequently labeled as "disruptive"—can reflect a heightened awareness of environmental details that others might miss.

Neurodiversity also highlights the importance of inclusivity and representation. When autistic voices are centered in conversations about policy, education, and media, society benefits from their unique insights. This book embraces the neurodiversity paradigm, aiming to celebrate autism as a valued part of human experience while addressing the barriers that can make life challenging for autistic individuals.

Breaking the Myths: What Autism Is and Isn't

Even as awareness of autism grows, myths and misconceptions persist. These falsehoods contribute to stigma, misunderstandings, and missed opportunities for connection and support. One pervasive myth is that all autistic individuals lack empathy. This idea stems from difficulties some autistic people may have in expressing emotions or interpreting social cues. However, research and lived experiences show that many autistic individuals feel empathy deeply—sometimes so intensely that it becomes overwhelming.

Another misconception is that autism always comes with intellectual disability. While some autistic individuals have intellectual challenges, many have average or above-average intelligence. Autism does not define someone's cognitive abilities but rather influences how they process and express information.

A third myth is that autistic individuals are antisocial or uninterested in relationships. The reality is more nuanced. While social interactions may be challenging, many autistic people deeply value connection and community. They may approach relationships differently but often bring honesty, loyalty, and authenticity to their interactions.

Finally, the idea that vaccines cause autism—debunked repeatedly by scientific studies—continues to harm public health and perpetuate stigma. Autism is not caused by vaccines but by a combination of genetic and environmental factors.

Chapter 2

The Spectrum and Beyond

Beyond the Diagnostic Criteria: Autism's Diverse Faces

Autism is often discussed through the lens of diagnostic checklists—challenges with social interaction, restricted interests, repetitive behaviors, and sensory sensitivities. While these traits are part of the story, they don't capture the full depth and breadth of how autism presents in individuals. Each autistic person is a unique blend of strengths, struggles, and adaptations shaped by their personality, environment, and life experiences.

One of the most significant revelations in recent years is how autism manifests differently across genders. For decades, autism research and diagnostic criteria were based primarily on studies of boys, leading to a gender bias in understanding the condition. Many autistic girls and women were overlooked because they often exhibit traits that differ from the stereotypical profile.

For instance, autistic girls might be more likely to mask or camouflage their traits, adapting their behavior to fit social norms. They may have intense interests, but instead of focusing on trains or technology *(often stereotyped as "male" interests)*, they might become deeply invested in animals, literature, or social dynamics. This ability to blend in can delay diagnosis, leaving many women to discover their autism later in life, often after years of misunderstanding and misdiagnosis.

Cultural differences also play a role in how autism is recognized and expressed. In some societies, the signs of autism may be attributed to personality traits, family dynamics, or even spirituality. A child who avoids eye contact might be seen as respectful rather than atypical, while repetitive behaviors could be viewed through a cultural or religious lens. These variations highlight the importance of culturally sensitive approaches to diagnosis and support.

The Many Ways Autism Manifests

Autism's diversity isn't just about how traits are expressed—it's also about how they evolve over time. An autistic child who struggles with verbal communication might grow into an adult with a rich vocabulary but prefer written over spoken interactions. Sensory sensitivities can shift, too; someone who finds loud noises unbearable in childhood might develop coping mechanisms as they age, though the underlying sensitivity remains.

The concept of spiky skill profiles is another hallmark of autism. Many autistic individuals have areas of exceptional ability alongside challenges in other domains. A person might excel in mathematics but find everyday executive functioning tasks, like organizing their schedule, incredibly difficult. Recognizing these uneven profiles is crucial for providing effective support and appreciating the full potential of autistic individuals.

Real-life examples bring these manifestations to life. Consider a young boy who communicates best through art, creating intricate drawings that speak volumes when words fail him. Or an autistic woman who thrives in a structured environment, using her ability to notice patterns to excel in data analysis. Then there's the nonverbal adult whose use of assistive technology allows them to share profound insights about their inner world. Each story adds a layer to our understanding of the spectrum's richness.

Embracing the Full Spectrum

To truly embrace autism, society must move beyond stereotypes and simplistic narratives. It's not enough to say *"If you've met one person with autism, you've met one person with autism."* We must also ask: What barriers prevent us from seeing the full spectrum? How can we create spaces where every autistic person feels valued and supported?

Part of the answer lies in education. Schools, workplaces, and communities must learn that autism is not a one-size-fits-all condition. Teachers need to understand that the quiet student who avoids group work isn't disengaged but might process information differently. Employers should recognize that an autistic employee's preference for routine and clear instructions isn't inflexibility but a strength that brings precision and reliability to their work.

Representation matters, too. Media often portrays autism through a narrow lens, focusing on either prodigious talent or profound disability. While these extremes are real, they leave out the majority of autistic experiences, which are nuanced and multifaceted. By amplifying diverse voices—autistic women, people of color, and individuals across the socioeconomic spectrum—we can reshape the public narrative to reflect autism's true breadth.

Finally, embracing the spectrum means celebrating its strengths while addressing its challenges. The ability to think differently, focus deeply, and perceive the world in unique ways are traits that enrich society. At the same time, we must ensure that autistic individuals have access to the tools and accommodations they need to thrive. Sensory-friendly environments, flexible communication methods, and acceptance of neurodiverse perspectives are just a few ways we can build a more inclusive world. Autism is not a single story; it's a collection of millions of stories, each as varied and valuable as the next. By acknowledging and embracing this diversity, we not only support autistic individuals but also deepen our collective humanity. The spectrum is vast, and its possibilities are limitless.

Chapter 3

The Voices of Autism

Personal Narratives: Real Stories from the Spectrum

The stories of autistic individuals offer profound insight into the diversity, resilience, and depth of human experience. These voices come from different corners of the spectrum, shedding light on the triumphs, struggles, and everyday realities of life as an autistic person.

Take, for instance, Emma, a young woman diagnosed with autism in her late twenties. For years, she struggled with overwhelming sensory input, often retreating into solitude to manage the chaos of her surroundings. After her diagnosis, she found a community of others who shared similar experiences. Now, Emma uses social media to advocate for sensory-friendly spaces and to help others feel less alone.

Then there's Malik, a nonverbal autistic man whose poetry, written with the help of an augmentative communication device, has captivated audiences worldwide. His words challenge assumptions about the inner lives of those who cannot speak traditionally. Malik reminds us that communication isn't confined to spoken words—it can be written, visual, or expressed through movement.

Each story is a window into the spectrum's complexity. From the teenager who uses video games to connect with others to the artist whose work captures the beauty of hyper-focused observation, these narratives paint a vivid picture of autism as lived experience.

Finding Identity and Belonging

Identity is a central theme for many autistic individuals. For some, receiving a diagnosis is a moment of clarity, a key that unlocks an understanding of themselves and their needs. It can be a relief to learn that what once felt isolating—preferences for routine, deep focus on specific interests, or struggles in social settings—has a name and a community.

Belonging often follows this discovery. Autistic individuals frequently find kinship in spaces where their traits are not just accepted but celebrated. Online forums, advocacy groups, and local meetups provide opportunities to connect, share experiences, and create friendships. These connections foster a sense of empowerment, reminding individuals that they are not alone and that their perspectives have value.

Identity can also mean reclaiming the narrative around autism. For years, society framed autism as a deficiency, focusing on what autistic people couldn't do. Today, many autistic voices are challenging that narrative, emphasizing the strengths and unique contributions of their community. This shift has led to greater acceptance and understanding, as well as a growing recognition of autism as a vital part of neurodiversity.

Voices That Challenge the Norm

The voices of autistic individuals are reshaping societal norms and expectations. Autistic advocates and creators are using their platforms to challenge outdated stereotypes, offering new perspectives on what it means to live on the spectrum.

Consider the work of Lydia X. Z. Brown, an activist who highlights the intersectionality of autism with race, gender, and disability rights. Their advocacy has sparked conversations about the additional challenges faced by autistic individuals in marginalized communities, pushing for a more inclusive understanding of neurodiversity.

Or think about Temple Grandin, whose pioneering work in animal behavior and advocacy for autistic individuals has inspired countless people. Her ability to explain her thought processes and sensory experiences has given the world a deeper appreciation for the autistic mind.

These voices also emphasize the need to rethink societal expectations. For example, the push for eye contact or "appropriate" social behavior often prioritizes neurotypical standards over autistic comfort and authenticity. By challenging these norms, autistic individuals are encouraging a broader acceptance of diverse ways of being.

Empowering Advocacy

The personal narratives and advocacy of autistic individuals have a ripple effect, inspiring others to champion neurodiversity. Readers of this chapter may feel moved to question their own assumptions about autism and to support initiatives that promote inclusivity.

Advocacy begins with listening. By amplifying autistic voices—whether through books, documentaries, or social media—we create a platform for understanding and acceptance. Advocacy also involves action: supporting policies that ensure accessibility, advocating for educational reforms, and challenging ableist attitudes in daily life.

Ultimately, these stories remind us that autism is not something to be fixed or cured—it's a way of experiencing the world. By valuing autistic voices and embracing their contributions, we enrich our communities and create a more inclusive society.

The voices of autism are as varied and vibrant as the spectrum itself. Each story holds the power to educate, challenge, and inspire. By listening to these voices, we take a crucial step toward a world where all neurodiverse individuals are seen, heard, and celebrated.

Chapter 4

The Science of Neurodiversity

Neurobiology of Autism: A Deeper Dive
Advancements in neuroscience have illuminated the intricate ways the autistic brain differs from neurotypical counterparts. Research has uncovered that autism is associated with variations in brain structure and function, particularly in regions responsible for sensory processing, communication, and social interaction. These differences are not defects but variations that contribute to the remarkable diversity of human cognition.

One key discovery involves neural connectivity. Many autistic individuals show either heightened or diminished connectivity between different brain regions. This can result in exceptional abilities in pattern recognition, memory, or detail-oriented tasks, while sometimes presenting challenges in multitasking or social comprehension.

Another area of focus is sensory processing. The autistic brain often processes sensory inputs with heightened sensitivity, which explains why environments that seem ordinary to others—like a bustling café or a fluorescent-lit office—can feel overwhelming. This heightened perception can also lead to unique strengths, such as an acute awareness of subtle details or changes that others might overlook.

The neurobiology of autism reminds us that these differences are not inherently positive or negative—they are simply part of the diverse ways humans experience the world. By embracing these findings, society can move away from stigmatizing neurodivergent traits and toward a greater understanding of their value.

The Strengths of Neurodivergent Minds

While public discourse often focuses on the challenges associated with autism, it's equally important to highlight the strengths. Neurodivergent minds are often wired for innovation, creativity, and intense focus—qualities that drive breakthroughs in various fields.

Consider the ability to hyperfocus, a trait many autistic individuals possess. This deep engagement allows for remarkable achievements in specialized areas, from scientific research to artistic creation. Famous historical figures believed to have exhibited autistic traits—like Nikola Tesla and Emily Dickinson—demonstrated how this focus could shape entire disciplines.

Autistic individuals are often exceptional problem-solvers, thanks to their ability to think outside the box and approach challenges from unique angles. In technology, for instance, autistic professionals are valued for their precision and analytical thinking. Organizations like Microsoft and SAP have launched neurodiversity hiring initiatives, recognizing that these traits enhance their teams.

Attention to detail is another hallmark strength. Whether it's a software engineer spotting elusive bugs in a codebase or an artist capturing intricate patterns in their work, the capacity to notice what others might miss is a powerful asset.

These strengths are not ancillary—they are central to what makes autistic individuals indispensable contributors to society. By focusing on these abilities, we create a narrative that empowers and uplifts.

How Neurodiversity Is Shaping Society

The growing embrace of neurodiversity is reshaping how organizations, communities, and industries operate. A neurodiversity-positive perspective doesn't just benefit autistic individuals; it enriches society as a whole.

In the workplace, neurodiversity initiatives are gaining momentum. Companies that prioritize hiring neurodivergent individuals report increased creativity, productivity, and innovation. These organizations adapt their environments—whether by offering quiet workspaces or flexible schedules—to meet diverse needs, fostering a culture of inclusion that benefits all employees.

Education is another area seeing transformation. Schools are increasingly shifting from rigid, one-size-fits-all models to curricula that recognize and nurture the diverse ways students learn. Programs designed for neurodivergent learners often benefit their neurotypical peers, too, by promoting empathy, flexibility, and collaborative problem-solving.

The arts and media are also playing a role in championing neurodiversity. Films, books, and documentaries that authentically portray autistic characters or feature the voices of autistic creators are helping to break down stereotypes and foster understanding. These representations are not just important for autistic individuals—they encourage society to celebrate cognitive diversity as a whole.

Scientific Breakthroughs Supporting Neurodiversity

Emerging research supports the shift toward a neurodiversity-positive framework. Studies on cognitive strengths in autism—such as enhanced visual processing, heightened sensory awareness, and superior pattern recognition—validate what many autistic individuals have long expressed about their abilities.

Recent breakthroughs in genetic research highlight the complex interplay of genes that contribute to autism. This complexity challenges outdated notions of autism as a single "condition" and instead positions it as a natural variation within human genetics.

Another area of interest is neuroplasticity—the brain's ability to adapt and change. This research underscores the importance of creating environments that accommodate neurodivergent needs. When autistic individuals are supported, their abilities flourish, benefiting not only themselves but also their communities.

The rise of interdisciplinary research combining neuroscience, psychology, and sociology has furthered our understanding of autism. By recognizing that autistic traits exist on a continuum shared by all humans, these studies emphasize the importance of inclusion.

The science of neurodiversity is more than an academic pursuit—it's a call to reimagine our world. By understanding the neurobiology of autism, valuing its unique strengths, and adapting our systems to be more inclusive, we create a society that thrives on diversity.

As this chapter demonstrates, autism is not just a diagnosis; it's a powerful reminder of the infinite ways in which human brains can work. The more we learn, the more we see how neurodivergent minds challenge assumptions, enrich lives, and shape a better future for everyone.

Chapter 5

The Role of Society in Shaping Autism

The Social Stigma: Past and Present

Societal stigma surrounding autism has long shaped the experiences of autistic individuals, often marginalizing their voices and limiting their opportunities. Historically, autism was viewed through a medical lens that emphasized deficits rather than differences. This framing led to isolation, misunderstanding, and even harmful treatments aimed at "curing" behaviors that were simply variations in neurodevelopment.

In the mid-20th century, the term "refrigerator mother" propagated the false and damaging notion that autism resulted from cold or neglectful parenting. Such theories not only ignored the biological basis of autism but also added an unfair burden of shame to families seeking support. The stigma perpetuated by these misconceptions pushed many autistic individuals into the shadows, with little recognition of their strengths or potential.

Today, while understanding has grown, stigma remains a persistent challenge. Autistic individuals often encounter barriers in education, employment, and social settings due to misconceptions about their abilities. Stereotypes—such as the belief that all autistic people are either savants or incapable of independence—continue to perpetuate exclusion.

However, a shift is occurring. As society gains a more nuanced understanding of autism, the conversation is moving from fear and ignorance to awareness and acceptance.

Shifting Perspectives: A Movement Toward Acceptance

Over the past few decades, advocacy movements have played a critical role in transforming how autism is perceived. Autistic individuals, parents, researchers, and allies have worked tirelessly to challenge outdated narratives and replace them with perspectives rooted in understanding and empowerment.

The neurodiversity movement, born in the 1990s, has been at the forefront of this transformation. It promotes the idea that autism is a natural variation of human diversity, not a disorder to be "fixed." This movement has reframed the conversation, focusing on strengths and accommodations rather than deficits and treatments. Autistic advocates, such as Dr. Temple Grandin and Lydia X. Z. Brown, have brought their lived experiences to the forefront, proving that autistic voices are vital to shaping the narrative.

Initiatives like World Autism Awareness Day and organizations such as the Autism Self-

Advocacy Network (ASAN) have also raised visibility and fostered global conversations. Public events, educational campaigns, and social media platforms have become spaces for amplifying autistic perspectives and breaking down stigma.

The Role of Media, Representation, and Language

Media plays a powerful role in shaping societal attitudes toward autism. Authentic representation of autistic characters in television, film, and literature can challenge stereotypes and foster empathy. Shows like *Atypical* and films like *Temple Grandin* have brought nuanced portrayals of autism to mainstream audiences, sparking conversations about neurodiversity.

Yet, representation in media is far from perfect. Too often, autistic characters are depicted as savants or portrayed through the lens of neurotypical creators who fail to capture the full spectrum of experiences. Authentic representation—crafted by autistic writers and actors—remains an essential step toward broader acceptance.

Language, too, is a crucial factor in shaping perceptions. The way we talk about autism influences how society values neurodivergent individuals. Terms like "high-functioning" and "low-functioning" oversimplify the complexity of autism, reducing individuals to labels rather than recognizing their unique needs and strengths. Many autistic people prefer identity-first language ("autistic person") over person-first language ("person with autism"), as it acknowledges autism as an integral part of who they are.

By adopting respectful and inclusive language, society can foster a culture that values diversity and rejects stigma.

How Society Can Foster Neurodiversity

To create a world where neurodivergent individuals thrive, society must take deliberate steps to foster inclusivity. This begins with education. Schools and workplaces should prioritize accommodations that empower autistic individuals to succeed. For example, sensory-friendly classrooms, flexible workspaces, and training programs for staff can create environments where neurodivergent people feel valued and supported.

Community initiatives also play a vital role. Local governments and organizations can promote autism-friendly events, provide resources for families, and ensure public spaces are accessible. Efforts to include autistic voices in decision-making processes ensure that policies and programs reflect their needs and perspectives.

Employers, too, have an opportunity to lead. Neurodiversity hiring programs not only support autistic employees but also benefit organizations by bringing fresh perspectives and innovative solutions to challenges. Companies like Microsoft and IBM have shown how creating inclusive workplaces can unlock the potential of neurodivergent talent.

At the individual level, fostering neurodiversity begins with empathy. Educating oneself about autism, challenging biases, and advocating for accommodations are ways anyone can contribute to a more inclusive society. Listening to autistic voices and amplifying their stories helps to build understanding and combat stigma.

Toward a More Inclusive Future

As society evolves, the role of inclusivity becomes increasingly vital. By addressing stigma, embracing diverse perspectives, and creating spaces where autistic individuals are respected and celebrated. we move closer to a world where everyone has the opportunity to thrive.

The work of fostering neurodiversity is not just about supporting autistic individuals—it's about enriching society as a whole. A world that values every brain's unique contributions is a world where innovation, empathy, and creativity can flourish without bounds.

Chapter 6

Autism in the Workplace

Autistic Strengths in Professional Environments

Autistic individuals bring a wealth of unique strengths to professional settings. Among these are exceptional attention to detail, heightened pattern recognition, and an ability to focus intensely on specific tasks. These attributes can be particularly valuable in roles that require precision, creativity, or innovative thinking. Industries such as technology, research, design, and quality control often benefit from these qualities.

For example, an autistic software developer might excel at identifying bugs in code due to their meticulous nature, while an autistic scientist might bring fresh insights to complex problems through their ability to analyze data from unconventional perspectives. Autistic employees are also known for their honesty, reliability, and strong sense of justice—traits that contribute to fostering ethical and accountable workplace cultures.

By leveraging these strengths, organizations can tap into a diverse talent pool that drives innovation and productivity.

Navigating Workplace Challenges

Despite their potential, autistic individuals often face significant barriers in the workplace. These challenges stem not from their abilities but from environments and practices that fail to accommodate their needs. Sensory sensitivities, difficulties with social interactions, and a lack of understanding from colleagues can create stress and hinder performance.

For instance, open office layouts with bright lights and constant noise can be overwhelming for autistic employees. Social norms, such as small talk or unstructured networking events, may feel confusing or unnecessary, leading to misunderstandings with coworkers or supervisors. The lack of clear instructions and feedback can also pose obstacles, as many autistic individuals thrive in structured and predictable settings.

To address these barriers, workplaces must embrace inclusive practices. This includes providing quiet spaces, offering flexible working arrangements, and implementing clear communication channels. Training programs for managers and staff can also help create a culture of empathy and understanding.

Success Stories: How Neurodiversity Drives Innovation

Organizations that embrace neurodiversity are setting examples of how inclusive practices can lead to remarkable outcomes. Companies like Microsoft, SAP, and Ernst & Young have established neurodiversity hiring programs designed to recruit and retain autistic talent. These programs focus on adjusting hiring processes—such as replacing traditional interviews with skills-based assessments—and offering ongoing support to employees.

Microsoft's Autism Hiring Program, for instance, has resulted in the recruitment of individuals who have made significant contributions to the company's technology development. Similarly, SAP's Autism at Work initiative has seen autistic employees excel in areas like data analysis, where their unique cognitive abilities bring new efficiencies and insights.

Startups and smaller businesses are also joining the movement. By valuing neurodivergent perspectives, they are not only fostering inclusivity but also driving creativity and problem-solving in ways that set them apart in competitive markets.

How Businesses and Organizations Benefit

Beyond individual contributions, neurodiverse teams can transform organizational culture and performance. Diverse perspectives challenge groupthink, fostering innovation and adaptability. A team that includes autistic employees, for example, might approach a project with fresh strategies that wouldn't have emerged from a more homogenous group.

Moreover, embracing neurodiversity can enhance a company's reputation, attracting top talent and demonstrating a commitment to social responsibility. Customers and clients increasingly seek partnerships with organizations that prioritize inclusivity and equity.

Inclusive workplaces also experience improved morale and engagement across all employees. When everyone feels valued and supported, productivity and loyalty increase, creating a positive cycle that benefits both individuals and the organization.

Building a More Inclusive Workplace

Creating truly inclusive workplaces requires a shift in mindset. Companies must move beyond mere compliance and actively seek ways to accommodate and celebrate neurodiverse talent. This includes:

- **Tailored Recruitment Processes:** Traditional interviews may not highlight the strengths of autistic candidates. Alternative methods, such as work trials or project-based assessments, can better showcase their abilities.
- **Onboarding and Mentorship:** Providing detailed onboarding programs and pairing new employees with mentors can ease transitions and foster connections.
- **Reasonable Accommodations:** Simple adjustments, such as noise-canceling headphones, modified schedules, or task-specific workflows, can make a significant difference in an autistic employee's success.

- **Continuous Learning:** Ongoing training for all staff ensures that inclusivity remains a priority and that everyone understands the value of neurodiversity.

Toward a Future of Inclusive Workplaces

By recognizing and addressing barriers, celebrating unique strengths, and implementing inclusive practices, workplaces can become engines of innovation and change. The inclusion of autistic individuals is not a charitable act—it's a strategic investment in the potential of human diversity.

As more organizations embrace neurodiversity, they pave the way for a future where everyone, regardless of how they think or perceive the world, has an equal opportunity to contribute and succeed. This shift benefits not just the workplace but society at large, reminding us all of the power of understanding, respect, and collaboration.

Chapter 7

Autism in Education

Rethinking Learning: Tailoring Education for Neurodiverse Minds

Traditional educational systems often prioritize conformity and standardized methods, making it difficult for neurodiverse students, including those with autism, to thrive. The one-size-fits-all approach doesn't account for the unique ways in which autistic students process information, interact with peers, or respond to stimuli. For example, some students may excel in visual learning but struggle with verbal instructions, while others may shine in independent projects but feel overwhelmed in group activities.

Tailoring education to meet neurodiverse needs involves recognizing and valuing these differences. Personalized learning plans, sensory-friendly classrooms, and flexible teaching methods can transform the educational experience. For instance, integrating technology such as apps and devices designed for visual learning can help autistic students better grasp complex concepts.

Beyond academics, fostering emotional and social development is equally crucial. Structured support for building communication skills, managing sensory sensitivities, and navigating social dynamics can empower autistic students to feel confident and capable in their educational environments.

Challenges in Traditional Education Systems

The rigidity of traditional education often presents significant hurdles for autistic students. Overcrowded classrooms, noisy environments, and an emphasis on rote learning can create overwhelming and unproductive settings. Behavioral misunderstandings frequently arise when teachers lack awareness of autism-related traits, such as sensory overload or difficulty transitioning between activities.

For example, an autistic student might appear uncooperative when they're actually struggling to adjust to sudden changes in routine. Without understanding or accommodations, this behavior may lead to unnecessary disciplinary actions or social isolation.

Additionally, standardized testing measures do not account for the diverse ways autistic students demonstrate intelligence and creativity. A student with exceptional artistic skills or a deep understanding of a specialized topic may find these strengths overlooked in favor of traditional metrics like test scores.

These challenges highlight the urgent need for systemic change to ensure that educational spaces nurture, rather than hinder, neurodiverse learners.

How Schools and Communities Can Be More Inclusive

Inclusive education starts with cultivating an environment where every student feels valued and supported. Schools can take several steps to achieve this:

- **Training Educators:** Providing teachers with comprehensive training on autism equips them to better understand and support neurodiverse students. This includes recognizing sensory needs, developing alternative teaching strategies, and fostering an inclusive classroom culture.
- **Flexible Curricula:** Introducing varied teaching methods, such as project-based learning, sensory breaks, and alternative

assessments, allows students to engage with material in ways that suit their strengths.

- **Sensory-Friendly Environments:** Simple adjustments, such as quieter spaces, natural lighting, and reduced visual clutter, can help create calming and focused learning environments.
- **Peer Education Programs:** Educating neurotypical students about autism fosters empathy and reduces bullying. Activities that promote collaboration and mutual understanding can build strong, inclusive peer relationships.

Communities also play a vital role in supporting neurodiverse learners. Local organizations, libraries, and extracurricular programs can create inclusive spaces where students can explore their interests and talents. For example, autism-friendly sports leagues or art workshops can provide enriching experiences outside the classroom.

Teachers and Parents: Collaborating for Success

The collaboration between educators and parents is essential in supporting autistic students. Parents bring invaluable insights into their child's needs, preferences, and triggers, while teachers offer professional expertise and an understanding of educational strategies. Together, they can craft Individualized Education Programs (IEPs) or accommodations tailored to the student's unique needs.

Open communication is key. Regular meetings, progress updates, and shared goals ensure that everyone involved is working toward the same outcomes. For instance, a parent may notice that their child learns best through hands-on activities, prompting the teacher to incorporate similar methods in the classroom.

By working together, parents and educators can create a cohesive support system that fosters both academic and personal growth for autistic learners.

Real-life stories illustrate the transformative power of inclusive education. One notable example is Alex, a nonverbal autistic student who struggled in a traditional classroom due to his need for alternative communication methods. After being introduced to augmentative and alternative communication (AAC) devices, Alex began excelling in subjects like math and science, demonstrating a talent that had previously gone unnoticed.

Similarly, Ella, an autistic high school student with a passion for writing, faced challenges with sensory overload in crowded classrooms. Through accommodations such as noise-canceling headphones and a quiet workspace, she gained the confidence to pursue her dream of publishing poetry, even winning awards for her work.

These stories remind us of the potential within every autistic student when provided with the right support and opportunities.

Inclusive education is not just about meeting legal or moral obligations—it's about recognizing the richness that neurodiverse minds bring to learning communities. When schools and communities embrace diversity, they not only empower autistic students but also enrich the experiences of all learners by fostering empathy, creativity, and collaboration.

By continuing to rethink traditional models and prioritize inclusivity, we can create a future where education celebrates every student's potential and paves the way for a more understanding and equitable society.

Chapter 8

Autism in Relationships

Navigating Friendships and Family Dynamics
Friendships and familial relationships are pivotal in everyone's life, yet for autistic individuals, they often take on unique complexities. The diverse ways in which autistic people communicate, process emotions, and engage socially can enrich relationships but also present challenges.

Friendships may evolve differently for autistic individuals. Some may prefer deep, one-on-one connections rather than broader social circles, valuing authenticity and shared interests over conventional small talk. Others might struggle to interpret social cues, leading to misunderstandings. For instance, what a neurotypical friend perceives as aloofness could be a reflection of sensory overload or the need for personal space.

In family settings, relationships can flourish when loved ones are attuned to the autistic individual's needs and strengths. Families who embrace open communication and adapt to individual preferences create environments of trust and mutual understanding. This might involve respecting sensory sensitivities, avoiding overwhelming social gatherings, or supporting an autistic family member's unique passions.

For families, education and empathy are key. Parents and siblings can strengthen bonds by learning about autism and seeking to understand how their loved one perceives the world. Patience, consistency, and clear communication often lead to more harmonious family dynamics.

Romantic Relationships: Challenges and Insights

Romantic relationships can be both deeply rewarding and challenging for autistic individuals. While the journey is unique for each person, common hurdles may include navigating unspoken social rules, expressing emotions, or interpreting the nuances of a partner's behavior.

For instance, some autistic individuals may struggle with the abstract nature of romantic gestures or find it challenging to balance their needs with their partner's. Yet, the same traits that pose challenges—like honesty, loyalty, and a deep sense of justice—are often the qualities that make autistic partners incredibly caring and dependable.

Open and direct communication is crucial in romantic relationships. Partners can strengthen their bond by creating a safe space for discussing needs, preferences, and boundaries without judgment. For example, instead of expecting an autistic partner to "read between the lines," clearly expressing emotions and desires helps build trust and understanding.

Romantic relationships also benefit from shared activities that align with an autistic individual's interests or sensory comfort. Whether it's quiet evenings spent reading together, engaging in a shared hobby, or exploring nature, these moments foster connection and intimacy.

Building Strong Support Networks

A robust support network is essential for autistic individuals to thrive in their personal and social lives. These networks often extend beyond immediate family and friends to include educators, mentors, therapists, and community groups.

Support networks provide encouragement during challenges and celebrate achievements. They also create opportunities for autistic individuals to connect with others who share similar experiences. For example, joining an autism-focused support group can offer a sense of belonging and reduce feelings of isolation.

For neurotypical friends and family members, being part of this support network requires a commitment to ongoing learning and advocacy.

Listening without judgment, advocating for inclusion, and standing against stigma are vital steps in fostering strong relationships.

Strategies for Strengthening Connections
Building and maintaining healthy relationships with autistic individuals involves mutual effort and understanding. Here are some strategies:

- **Practice Empathy:** Seek to understand how the autistic person perceives and experiences the world. Asking questions like, "How can I support you better?" demonstrates care and builds trust.

- **Prioritize Clear Communication:** Autistic individuals often appreciate straightforward and honest dialogue. Avoid ambiguous phrases or expecting them to infer meaning from subtle cues.

- **Respect Boundaries:** Autistic people may need time alone to recharge, especially after social interactions. Respecting this need without taking it personally strengthens relationships.

- **Learn Together:** Explore resources on autism, attend workshops, or participate in autism-focused events as a team. This shared learning journey fosters connection and empathy.
- **Celebrate Strengths:** Recognize and appreciate the unique qualities that an autistic individual brings to the relationship, such as creativity, focus, or a fresh perspective on life.

Shaping a More Inclusive Future

Strong relationships between autistic and neurotypical individuals enrich both parties and pave the way for a more inclusive society. When friendships, families, and communities embrace neurodiversity, they foster environments where everyone feels valued.

This chapter invites readers to challenge preconceived notions about relationships and autism, embrace empathy, and take meaningful steps toward building connections that honor the individuality and humanity of all.

Chapter 9

The Future of Autism Awareness

Changing Perceptions and Creating Space for Neurodivergence

The world is shifting toward a broader understanding of what it means to be autistic. Historically, misconceptions and stigma shaped public perception, but the tide is turning. Neurodiversity advocacy emphasizes that autistic individuals are not defined solely by challenges but by their diverse strengths and contributions.

For this progress to continue, society must challenge entrenched biases and reframe autism as a natural variation of the human experience. Public policies need to reflect this shift, prioritizing inclusion over assimilation. Education systems, workplaces, and community programs must adopt approaches that empower autistic individuals rather than pressuring them to conform to neurotypical norms.

Creating space for neurodivergence also requires accessible platforms for autistic voices. The perspectives of autistic individuals should guide decisions about autism-related services, policies, and representation. By amplifying these voices, society can learn to appreciate the depth and richness that neurodiverse minds contribute.

The Role of Technology and Innovation in Autism Care

Technology is revolutionizing the way autism is understood and supported. Innovative tools are breaking down barriers and opening new possibilities for communication, learning, and independence.

For instance, assistive communication devices have empowered non-speaking autistic individuals to express their thoughts and emotions more effectively. Apps designed for emotional regulation and social skills training are making it easier for autistic people to navigate complex interactions. Virtual reality environments are being used to create safe spaces where individuals can practice social scenarios at their own pace.

Beyond personal tools, data-driven research is providing valuable insights into autism. Machine learning algorithms are helping identify patterns in behavior and brain activity, leading to earlier and more accurate diagnoses. Wearable technology is enabling real-time monitoring of sensory overload or stress levels, allowing for timely interventions.

However, it is essential that these technologies are developed in collaboration with the autism community. Input from autistic individuals ensures that innovations meet real needs and avoid perpetuating stereotypes or exclusionary practices.

The Global Movement for Neurodiversity

The neurodiversity movement is gaining momentum worldwide, uniting individuals, families, educators, and advocates in a shared vision of inclusion. This grassroots effort challenges the medical model of autism, which often focuses on "fixing" or "curing" differences, and instead embraces the idea that diversity strengthens humanity.

Global advocacy groups are working to dismantle stigma and advocate for the rights of neurodivergent individuals. Campaigns like World Autism Awareness Day and organizations such as the Autism Self-Advocacy Network are raising awareness and promoting policies that support autistic people in every aspect of life.

This movement is also fostering cross-cultural collaboration. While the experiences of autism vary across different societies, the call for acceptance and understanding transcends borders. Sharing best practices and learning from diverse perspectives enriches the global conversation about neurodiversity.

A Vision for an Inclusive Future

Imagine a world where neurodiversity is not merely accepted but celebrated. In this future, public policies ensure that autistic individuals have equitable access to education, healthcare, and employment. Workplaces actively seek out neurodivergent talent, valuing the creativity, focus, and unique perspectives that autistic minds offer.

In this vision, classrooms are equipped with tools that cater to diverse learning styles, and teachers receive training to support neurodivergent students effectively. Media representation reflects the authenticity and breadth of autistic experiences, challenging stereotypes and inspiring greater empathy. Communities would prioritize universal design, creating spaces that are welcoming for all sensory needs. Quiet areas in public spaces, sensory-friendly events, and accessible communication tools would become the norm rather than the exception.

This future also values continuous dialogue and learning. As science and society evolve, so too does the understanding of autism. The goal is not to reach a definitive conclusion but to remain open to growth and adaptation.

Lighting the Path Forward

The journey toward widespread autism acceptance and inclusion requires collective effort. Policymakers, educators, healthcare providers, employers, and community members all have roles to play. By prioritizing understanding, embracing innovation, and supporting global advocacy, society can move closer to a world where neurodiversity is truly embraced.

This chapter invites readers to take part in shaping this future. Whether through advocacy, education, or personal connections, every action contributes to a brighter and more inclusive tomorrow. Together, we can ensure that the world not only makes space for neurodivergence but thrives because of it.

Conclusion

Embracing Neurodiversity

The journey of understanding autism and embracing neurodiversity is not just about awareness—it's about transformation. It requires a shift in how society perceives differences and values the contributions of every individual. Autism is not a limitation; it's a variation of the human experience that enriches our collective potential.

Creating a more inclusive world means dismantling barriers that hold back autistic individuals. This is not charity—it's equity. Inclusive policies, accessible environments, and authentic representation in media and leadership are essential for everyone to thrive. Acceptance isn't a single act; it's an ongoing commitment to fairness, kindness, and understanding.

For readers inspired to make a difference, the next steps begin with action. Advocacy can take many forms—speaking out against harmful stereotypes, supporting neurodivergent colleagues or loved ones, or participating in community efforts to make spaces more accessible.

Education is a powerful tool. Learn about the challenges autistic individuals face and the strengths they bring to the table. Share this knowledge with others to shift mindsets and build bridges of understanding. Seek out and amplify the voices of autistic self-advocates. Their experiences and insights provide invaluable perspectives that shape how society evolves.

Empathy is the foundation of this change. Understanding someone else's reality—listening, learning, and responding with compassion—is how inclusion takes root. Empathy isn't about pity; it's about respect. It's about creating a world where everyone feels seen and valued.

Final Thoughts: Redefining What It Means to Be Autistic

Autism is not something to be fixed or feared—it's something to be understood and appreciated. By redefining what it means to be autistic, we challenge outdated ideas that limit potential and perpetuate stigma. Autistic individuals bring creativity, focus, authenticity, and unique problem-solving skills that can inspire new ways of thinking and doing.

The vision for the future is clear: a society where differences are celebrated, where inclusion is a standard, and where neurodiversity drives innovation and growth. A world where being autistic is seen not as a challenge but as a contribution to the richness of humanity.

This book is not the final word on autism or neurodiversity—it's an invitation. It's a call to continue the conversation, take action, and build communities that thrive on diversity. Each reader has the power to make a difference, whether through advocacy, creating inclusive spaces, or simply showing understanding and support in daily life.

The future is ours to shape. Let's move toward a world where everyone—autistic or otherwise—has the opportunity to shine. By embracing neurodiversity, we unlock the potential for a brighter, more compassionate, and more innovative tomorrow.

Acknowledgements

I am deeply grateful to the many people who have contributed to this book in ways both large and small. Without your input, guidance, and support, this work would not have come to life in the way it has.

To the autistic individuals who shared their stories—your courage and vulnerability have been my greatest inspiration. Your voices, your experiences, and your truth shape the essence of this book. I am honored to have had the opportunity to amplify your words.

To the researchers, educators, and advocates in the neurodiversity movement: Your work has not only enlightened me but also countless others. Your tireless efforts to shift perspectives and build a more inclusive society deserve to be acknowledged and celebrated.

To my friends and family, thank you for your unwavering support. Your belief in me, in this project, and in the importance of challenging societal norms has meant the world.

To the individuals who may have been skeptical or unsure, thank you for pushing me to think harder, deeper, and more critically. Your questions have helped shape this work into something meaningful.

Finally, to the readers who open these pages, I hope this book leaves you with a deeper understanding of autism and neurodiversity and a renewed commitment to building a world that embraces all minds. Your willingness to learn, grow, and advocate is the key to making the future more inclusive and equitable for everyone.

www.ingramcontent.com/pod-product-compliance
Lightning Source LLC
Chambersburg PA
CBHW050817250726
48653CB00006B/2277